Anthems
for Choirs
1

50 anthems for mixed voices

Edited by
FRANCIS JACKSON

Oxford University Press

Music Department Walton Street Oxford OX2 6DP

Preface

These fifty anthems have been chosen with average parish church choirs in mind, but it is hoped that the collection will prove useful to cathedrals, collegiate churches, and those parish churches supporting cathedral-type choirs. Anthems suitable for unaccompanied singing and those needing organ accompaniments are about equal in number; most are for four voices (S.A.T.B.) without *divisi* parts.

Four anthems have been written specially for the book by Francis Jackson, Kenneth Leighton, David Lord, and William Mathias; other composers represented date from the first half of the sixteenth century to the present day.

The collection covers all the main seasons and festivals of the Church's Year, and also includes twenty-one anthems for general use.

Index of Titles and First Lines

Where first lines differ from titles the former are shown in italics.

Anthems suitable for unaccompanied singing are marked thus *
Anthems in not more than four parts throughout are marked thus †

continued overleaf

Seasonal Index

Index of Composers and Arrangers

1. A SOUND OF ANGELS

(A Christmas song)

Edited by W. M. ATKINS
Words by W. M. A.

CHRISTOPHER TYE
(c. 1500-1572 or 1573)

Christopher Tye, Mus. D., lay clerk of King's College, Cambridge, was appointed Master of Choristers at Ely Cathedral in 1541, a position which he held till 1561 when he was appointed Rector of Doddington, having entered on Holy Orders in the previous year. He composed much fine music for the Roman rite, but his true importance lies in the formative influence he exercised on the music of the reformed liturgy. His only work published in his lifetime was **The Actes of the Apostles, translated into Englyshe Metre,** of which two editions appeared in 1553. Only the first fourteen chapters were printed, each having a setting for four voices. Tye's verses are deplorable doggerel, but much of the music to them is so excellent that alternative words have several times been supplied, and it is in the hope that the charming setting to Chapter VI of the **Actes** may be more widely known that this edition has been made. W.M.A.

This anthem is published separately (O. U. P. OM 22).

2. AH, THOU POOR WORLD

Edited by W. GILLIES WHITTAKER
Words anon. tr. ALBERT G. LATHAM

JOHANNES BRAHMS Op. 110, No. 2
(1833-1897)

6 (15)   *D.C.*

plea - sure, Yet in thee seek my plea - - - sure.
mea - sure, Thy joys have brief - est mea - - - sure.

plea - sure, Yet in thee seek my plea - - - sure.
mea - sure, Thy joys have brief - est mea - - - sure.

plea - sure, Yet in thee seek_ my plea - sure, seek_ my plea - sure.
mea - sure, Thy joys have brief - est mea - sure, brief-est mea - sure.

plea - sure, Yet in thee seek_ my plea - sure, seek_ my plea - sure.
mea - sure, Thy joys have brief - est mea - sure, brief-est mea - sure.

6 (15)   *D.C.*

19
f sempre

3. Thy wealth, thine hon - ours man - i - fold, In need,_ in death, no

f sempre
3. Thy wealth, thine hon - ours man - i - fold,_ In need, in death,_ no

f sempre
3. Thy wealth, thine hon- ours man - i - fold,_ In need,_ in death,_ no

f sempre
3. Thy wealth, thine hon - ours man - i - fold,_ In need, in death, no

19

f

com - fort hold, Thy gold_ is naught but tin - sel gold, Be thou, O Lord, my

com - fort hold, Thy gold is naught but tin - sel gold, Be thou, O Lord, my

com - fort hold,_Thy gold_ is naught_but_ tin - sel gold, Be thou, O Lord, my

com - fort hold,_Thy gold is naught but tin - sel gold, Be thou, O Lord, my

trea - sure, Be thou, O Lord, my trea - - - sure.

trea - sure, Be thou, O Lord, my trea - - - sure.

trea-sure, Be thou, O Lord,_ be thou,_ O Lord,_my trea - sure.

trea-sure, Be thou, O Lord,_ be thou,_ O Lord,_my trea - sure.

3. SOLUS AD VICTIMAM

Words by
PETER ABELARD (1079-1142)
Tr. HELEN WADDELL

KENNETH LEIGHTON

A - lone— to sac - ri-fice thou go-est, Lord,—

Gi-ving thy-self to Death whom thou hast slain.— For us thy wret-ched folk

The words are reprinted by permission of the Executor to the late Helen Waddell.

is a-ny word?__ Who know that for our sins__ this is thy pain?__

cresc. poco

mf

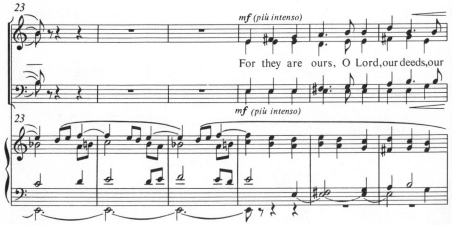

For they are ours, O Lord, our deeds, our

mf (più intenso)

deeds,__ Why must thou suf - fer tor-ture for our sin?__

(Ped.)

Let our hearts suf-fer in thy Pas - sion, Lord,— That ve-ry suf-fer-ing

may— thy mer - cy win.— This is the night— of

tears,— the three— days' space,— Sor-row a - bi-ding of the e - ven-tide,—

(Ped.)

Un-til the day break with the ri - sen Christ, And hearts that sor- rowed shall be

sa - tis -fied.   So may our hearts share in thine an - guish, Lord,—

That   they   may   sha - rers   of thy   glo - ry__   be;—

* Altos may sing an 8ve lower in this phrase if desired.

Hea-vy with weep-ing may the three days pass, To win the

To win the

laugh - ter, the laugh - - - - - ter of thine

laugh - - - ter, the laugh - - - ter of thine

(Man.)

Eas - ter Day.

Eas - ter Day.

Ped.

4. ALL PEOPLE THAT ON EARTH DO DWELL

Edited by
ANTHONY GREENING

Attributed to
THOMAS TALLIS
(c. 1505 - 1585)

Words: W. Kethe, Day's Psalter (1560-1)

© Oxford University Press 1973

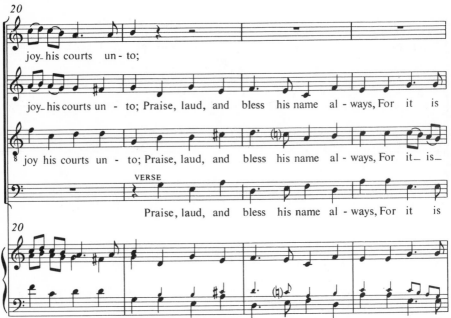

His truth hath al - ways firm - ly stood, And shall from

sure; His truth hath al - ways firm - ly stood, And shall from

is for ev - er_ sure; His truth_ hath_al - ways firm - ly stood, And

is for ev - er sure; His truth hath al - ways firm - ly stood, And

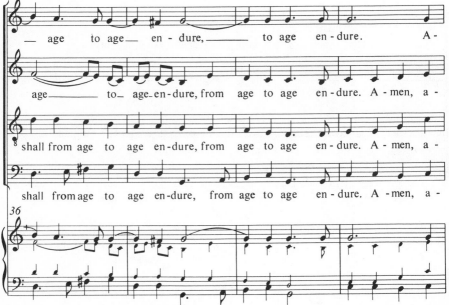

_ age to age_ en - dure,____ to age en - dure. A -

age____ to_ age_en - dure, from age to age en - dure. A - men, a -

shall from age to age en - dure, from age to age en - dure. A - men, a -

shall from age to age en - dure, from age to age en - dure. A - men, a -

1. **Sources:** all in Christ Church Library, Oxford:—

A   Ms 11
B   Ms 16, pp. 1-2
C   Ms 16, pp. 46-47   } full vocal scores
D   Ms 614
E   Ms 1230   } organ books
F   Ms 1235
G   Mss 1221-1224   } Tenor and bass
     [pp. 200, 190, 188, 186]   part-books

2. **Editorial practice:**
Small notes and cautionary accidentals in brackets
are editorial. Note values halved: pitch unaltered.

3. **Ascription:**
Although ascribed to Tallis in the sources, this anthem would seem to be an adaptation by Dean Al-
drich. On stylistic grounds alone the ascription
seems dubious.

4. **Variants:**
Another version of this anthem is to be found in Mss
1220-1224 [pp. 184, 179, 173, 173, 168]. It is a
setting of the first and fourth verses of the hymn only
to the music of the full sections here presented. Its in-
completeness precludes its listing as a variant. Source
C only contains a different setting of the third verse
of the hymn, which cannot be reproduced here for
lack of space.

Source	/	bar	/	stave	/	beat	/	variant
C	/	2	/	1	/	4	/	crotchet E
C	/	2	/	2	/	3-4	/	crotchet G,
								crotchet C
C	/	10	/	1	/	3-4	/	dotted crotchet,
								quaver
D	/	12	/	3	/	2	/	flat to B
C	/	27	/	1	/	3-4	/	two crotchets
C & D	/	28	/	4	/	3-4	/	two crotchets
C	/	29	/	2	/	3	/	quaver D,
								quaver E
C	/	31	/	2	/	3-4	/	quavers E F E D
D & B	/	31	/	3	/	2-3-4	/	underlay: 'His
								mercy is'
C	/	37	/	3 & 4	/	1-2	/	dotted crotchets,
								quavers

To the Rev. F. Harrison

5. ALMIGHTY GOD, THE FOUNTAIN OF ALL WISDOM

A Collect

ERNEST FARRAR
(1885-1918)

Al-migh-ty God, the foun-tain of all wis-dom,

who know-est our ne - ces - si-ties be - fore we

ask, and our ig - nor-ance in ask - ing; We be -

to have com-pas - sion up - on our in-firm - it - ies;

-seech thee have com-pas - sion up - on our in-firm - it - ies;

6. ALMIGHTY GOD, WHICH HAST ME BROUGHT

Words by
SIR WILLIAM LEIGHTON

THOMAS FORD (c. 1580-1648)
edited by Nicholas Steinitz

This piece comes from Sir William Leighton's **The Teares or Lamentacions of a Sorrowfull Soule,** 1614, for which it was probably specially written. The cantus and lute parts are found in Royal App. 63, and reference has been made to an 18th-century transcription in Add. 31418. In the original edition the cantus was doubled with treble viol, the alto with 'flute' (i.e. recorder), and the bass with bass viol. Lute, citterne, and bandora tablatures were also provided. Although these are a most interesting feature of the composition and are useful in elucidating doubtful points in the text, they are in this case little more than a plain reduction of the voice parts, and it is suggested that the short score will generally prove an adequate accompaniment if one is needed.

The original barring (present in all parts except the bass) has been preserved as far as possible. Cautionary accidentals in brackets and slurs are editorial. Accidentals present originally but not required in modern notation have been omitted.

N.S.

* Printed as A, but corrected to G by hand in the British Museum copy.

to   this   pre-sent day,   Keep me from sin in heart and thought, and
thy   con - tin-ual grace,   Keep me from Sa-tan vile that lurks to
heart   and   guide my ways,   A - mend my miss, my mind re - move from

to   this pre - sent day,   Keep me from sin in heart   and _____ thought, and
thy   con - tin- ual grace,   Keep me from Sa-tan vile   that _____ lurks to
heart   and guide   my ways,   A-mend my miss, my mind   re - move from

to this pre   -   sent day,   Keep me from sin   in heart and thought, and
thy con-tin - ual grace,   Keep me from Sa   -   tan vile that lurks to
heart and guide   my ways,   A-mend my miss,   my mind re-move from

to   this present day,   Keep   me from sin in heart and thought, and
thy   con-tin-ual grace,   Keep   me from Sa-tan vile that lurks to
heart   and guide my ways,   A   -   mend my miss, my mind re-move from

1st time for each verse   *10*   D.S. 2nd time for each verse

teach   me_ what   to   do and say.   Keep   do and say.
trap   my_ soul   in   ev-'ry place.   Keep   ev-'ry place.
all   that_ from thy glo-ry strays.   A -   glo-ry strays.

teach_ me   what_ to   do and say. Keep   me   from   do and say.
trap_ my   soul_ in   ev-'ry place. Keep   me   from   ev-'ry place.
all ____ that   from_ thy   glo-ry strays. A - mend   my   glo-ry strays.

teach   me_ what   to   do and say. Keep   me   from   do and say.
trap   my_ soul   in   ev-'ry place. Keep   me   from   ev-'ry place.
all   that_ from thy   glo-ry strays. A - mend   my   glo-ry strays.

teach_ me   what_ to   do and say.   Keep   do and say.
trap_ my   soul_ in   ev-'ry place.   Keep   ev-'ry place.
all ____ that   from_ thy   glo-ry strays.   A - - - glo-ry strays.

1st time for each verse   *mp* D.S. 2nd time for each verse

dim.   *mp*
              (♮)d

† G omitted through printer's error, but added by hand in Br. Mus. copy and R.A. 63 and confirmed in the tablatures.

* Originally there was a third in the accompaniment only, so altos can sing B natural here if the piece is performed unaccompanied.

7. SONG 46
(CHRISTMAS DAY)

Edited by FRANCIS JACKSON

ORLANDO GIBBONS
(1583-1625)

1. As on the night before this bless-ed morn, A troop of angels unto shepherds told, Where

2. This favour Christ vouchsafed for our sake: To buy us thrones he in a manger lay; Our

Source: *Hymns and Songs of the Church*, George Wither (London 1623).

© Oxford University Press 1973

in a sta - ble he was poor - ly born, Whom nor the earth, nor
weak-ness took, that we his strength might take, And was dis-rob'd that

heav'n of heav'ns can hold. Through Beth - lem rung this
he might us ar - ray: Our flesh he wore, our

news at their re - turn; Yea, an - gels sung that
sin to wear a - way: Our curse he bore, that

news at their re - turn; Yea, an - gels sung that
sin to wear a - way: Our curse he bore, that

news at their re - turn; Yea, an - gels sung that
sin to wear a - way: Our curse he bore, that

news at their re - turn; Yea, an - gels sung that
sin to wear a - way: Our curse he bore, that

GOD WITH US was born: And they made mirth be - -
we es - cape it may; And wept for us, that

GOD WITH US was born: And they made mirth be - -
we es - cape it may; And wept for us, that

GOD WITH US was born: And they made mirth be - -
we es - cape it may; And wept for us, that

GOD WITH US was born: And they made mirth be - -
we es - cape it may; And wept for us, that

Original key: F. The treble and bass only are original; alto and tenor parts, vocal slurring, and the optional organ part are editorial. Barring has been modernized. Cautionary accidentals are placed in brackets.

8. AWAKE US, LORD, AND HASTEN

(ERTÖDT' UNS DURCH DEIN' GÜTE)

from Cantata 22

Words by C. S. TERRY

J. S. BACH
(1685-1750)
adapted by Francis Jackson

* Small notes are optional alternatives for pedalling.

Bright registration is suggested — a combination which includes two-foot stops and mutations. The right hand should predominate over the left. When it is desired to play the accompaniment without pedals the middle stave of the organ part may be omitted; the left hand can then be played either on the same manual as the right or on a second manual, with or without sixteen-foot tone.

The English words are from **Bach Cantata Texts Sacred and Secular** (Terry) and are used by permission of Constable & Co.

5 (14)

-wake_ us,_ Lord,_ and_ hast - en!
old_ man_ in _ us_ chast - en,

8(17)   *D.S.*

Thy   Ho - ly   Spi - rit_ give!
That   our_ new man_ may_ live,

9. BEHOLD, HOW GOOD AND JOYFUL

Psalm 133

JOHN CLARKE-WHITFELD
(1770-1836)

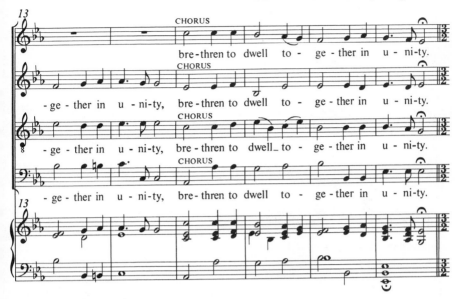

bre-thren to dwell to - ge - ther in u - ni-ty.

- ge - ther in u - ni-ty, bre-thren to dwell to - ge - ther in u - ni-ty.

- ge - ther in u - ni-ty, bre-thren to dwell_ to - ge - ther in u - ni-ty.

- ge - ther in u - ni-ty, bre-thren to dwell to - ge - ther in u - ni-ty.

Andante
BASS SOLO *19*

It is like the pre-cious oint - ment up - on the head,__ that ran

down__ un-to the beard, ev'n un-to Aa-ron's beard, ev'n un-to

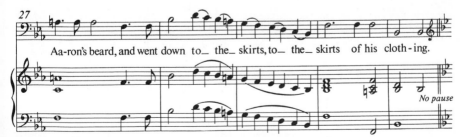

Aa-ron's beard, and went down to__ the__ skirts, to__ the__ skirts of his cloth-ing.

No pause

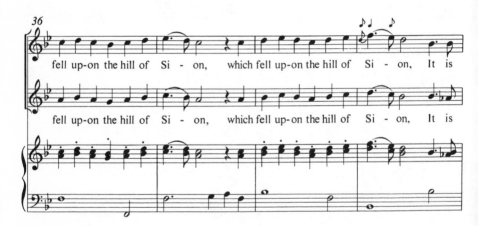

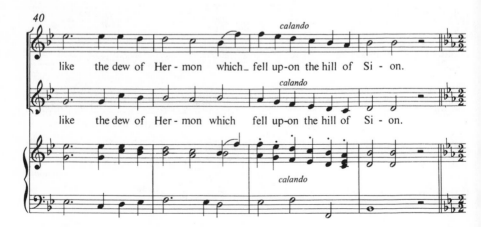

pro-mis-ed his bless-ing,   and
pro-mis-ed his bless-ing,   and life for ev-er-
pro-mis-ed his bless-ing,   and life for ev-er-more,   and life for ev-er-
pro-mis-ed his bless-ing, and life for ev-er-more,   and life for ev-er-more,   and

life for ev-er-more, for_ ev-er, ev - er - more.   For there the   Lord
- more,   and life   for_ ev - er - more.   For there   the_ Lord pro -
- more,   and life   for_ ev - er - more.   For there   the   Lord
life for ev-er-more,   for_ ev - er - more.   For there   the   Lord

10. CANTATE DOMINO
(COME YE WITH JOYFULNESS)

English words by
FRANCIS JACKSON

GIUSEPPE OTTAVIO PITONI
(1657-1743)
Edited by R.R.TERRY

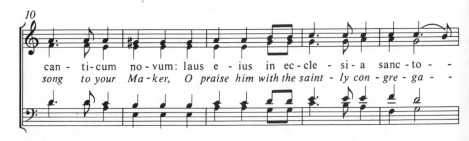

This edition of the music and Latin text is used by permission of L.J.Cary & Co. Ltd.
The words are paraphrased from Psalm 148.

© Oxford University Press 1973 (English text)

11. SONG 44
(VENI CREATOR)

Edited by FRANCIS JACKSON

ORLANDO GIBBONS
(1583-1625)

Source: *Hymnes and Songs of the Church*, George Wither (London 1623).

© Oxford University Press 1973

had be - ing from, Oh, fill them with   thy heav'n- ly

____ had be - ing from, Oh, fill____ them   with thy heav'n - ly

had be - ing_ from, Oh, fill   them with   thy hea - - ven - ly

had be - ing   from,   Oh, fill them with   thy heav'n- ly

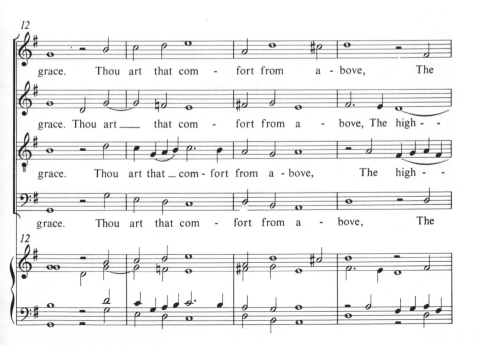

grace. Thou art that com - fort from   a - bove,   The

grace. Thou art____ that com - fort from a - bove, The high - -

grace.   Thou art that _ com - fort from a - bove,   The high - -

grace.   Thou art that com - fort from a - bove,   The

Original key: F. The treble and bass only are original; alto and tenor parts, vocal slurring, and the optional organ part are editorial. Barring has been modernized. Bar 17: bass rhythm originally two semibreves.

12. FROM THE RISING OF THE SUN

Malachi I, v.11

F. A. GORE OUSELEY
(1825 - 1889)

9
mf
-tiles; and in ev - - 'ry place, and in ev - - 'ry place in-cense
mf
-tiles; and in ev - - 'ry place, and in ev - - 'ry place in - cense
mf
-tiles; and in ev - - 'ry place, and in ev - - 'ry place in - cense
mf
-tiles; and in ev - - 'ry place,_and in ev - - 'ry place in - cense
9
mf

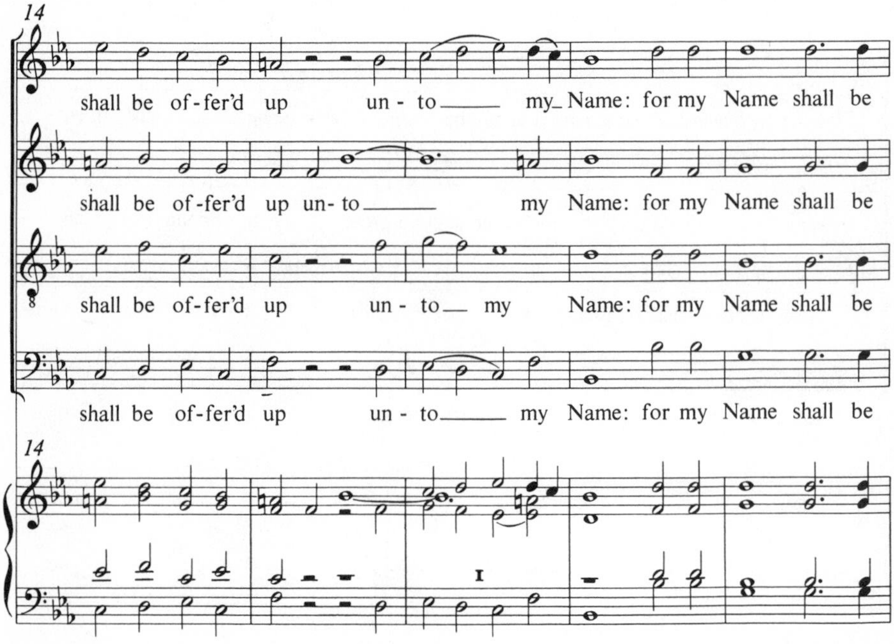
14
shall be of-fer'd up un - to_ my_Name: for my Name shall be
shall be of-fer'd up un- to_ my Name: for my Name shall be
shall be of-fer'd up un - to_ my Name: for my Name shall be
shall be of-fer'd up un - to_ my Name: for my Name shall be
14

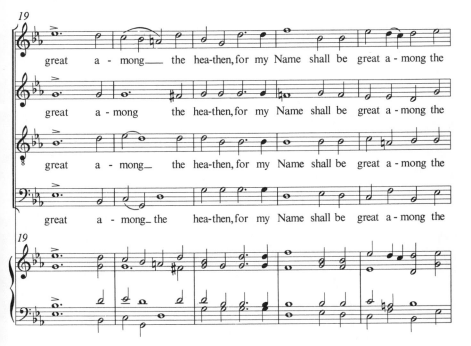

great a - mong___ the hea-then, for my Name shall be great a - mong the

great a - mong the hea-then, for my Name shall be great a - mong the

great a - mong___ the hea-then, for my Name shall be great a - mong the

great a - mong_ the hea-then, for my Name shall be great a - mong the

hea - - then, thus saith the Lord! thus saith the Lord!

hea - - then, thus saith the Lord! thus saith the Lord!

hea - - then, thus___ saith the Lord! thus___ saith the Lord!

hea - - then, thus saith the Lord! thus saith the Lord!

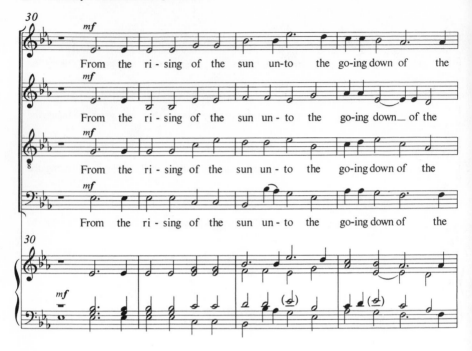

From the ri - sing of the sun un-to the go-ing down of the
From the ri - sing of the sun un - to the go-ing down__ of the
From the ri - sing of the sun un - to the go-ing down of the
From the ri - sing of the sun un - to the go-ing down of the

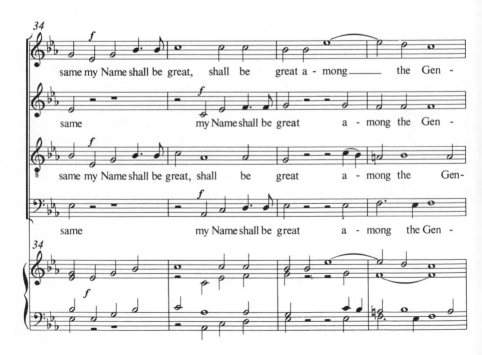

same my Name shall be great, shall be great a - mong_____ the Gen -
same my Name shall be great a - mong the Gen -
same my Name shall be great, shall be great a - mong the Gen-
same my Name shall be great a - mong the Gen -

-tiles; and in ev - 'ry place, and in ev - 'ry place in-cense

-tiles; and in ev - 'ry place, and in ev - 'ry place in-cense

-tiles; and in ev - 'ry place, and in ev - 'ry place in-cense

-tiles; and in ev - 'ry place,_and in ev - 'ry place in-cense

shall be of-fer'd up   un - to____ my Name, thus ____   saith the Lord.

shall be of-fer'd up un-to ____   my Name, thus ____ saith the Lord.

shall be of-fer'd up   un - to__ my__ Name, thus__ saith__ the Lord.

shall be of-fer'd up   un - to____ my Name, thus   saith   the   Lord.

13. GIVE ALMES OF THY GOODS

Edited by ANTHONY GREENING
Offertory sentence, B.C.P.
from Tobit 4

CHRISTOPHER TYE
(c. 1500-1572 or 1573)

* The E♭ in the source conflicts with the D♭ in both organ parts, and seems to the editor to be a manifest error on the part of the scribe.

This anthem is published separately (O.U.P. TCM57 revised).

© Oxford University Press 1972

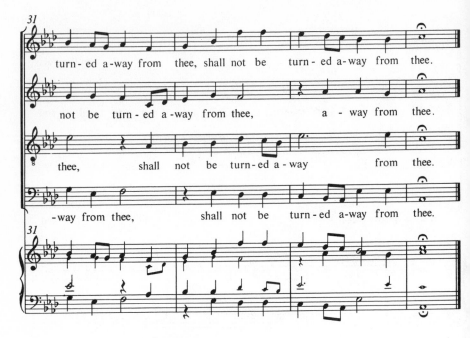

1. Sources:
A   British Museum, Add. Mss 30480-3; four part-books late 16th cent.
B   University of California, Berkeley, Ms M2 C645 case B; an organ part early 17th cent.
C   Christ Church Library, Oxford, Ms 88; an organ part late 17th cent.
D   St Michael's College, Tenbury, Ms 1442; a bass part-book c. 1669.
E   Wimborne Minster Library, Mss P11, 14, 15, 17; alto, tenor and two bass part-books c. 1670.

2. Variants:
Sources D and E both set 'alms' as a single syllable on a minim.

Source	bar	stave	beat	variant
E	5	4	4	D flat
E	6	2	3-4	dotted crotchet A flat, semi-quavers G and F for 'thy'
E	11	2	3½	semiquavers A flat, B flat
E	16	2	2-3-4	minim F, crotchet E natural
E	25-26	2	4-1-2	minim F, crotchet E natural
B	18	5	3	quavers A flat, B flat in alto
B	22	6	3	crotchet E flat in place of rest

3. Editorial practice:
Small notes in the organ part and the crossed slur are editorial.

14. GOD IS OUR HOPE AND STRENGTH

Edited by H. P. ALLEN

J. S. BACH
(1685-1750)

1. God is our hope and strength,
2. Hon-our and thanks to God,

All heav'n and earth a - -
Who wrought this world's cre - -

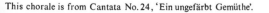

This chorale is from Cantata No. 24, 'Ein ungefärbt Gemüthe'.

And_ pros-trate fall_ be - fore____ him!
In ___ death_ and tri - bu - la - - tion.

For_ all things are____ of_ him,
Him_ praise we_ while_ we_ live,

And   in   all____ things__ is__
And   on   his____ will__ at -

is
at -

he,
- tend,

The__ works that aye__ have__
Un - til__ we_there_ar -

he,
-tend,

mf   *cresc.*

15. HASTE THEE, O GOD

Edited by ANTHONY GREENING

ADRIAN BATTEN
(1591-1637)

Psalm 70; vv. 1-4

This anthem is published separately (TCM 78 revised).

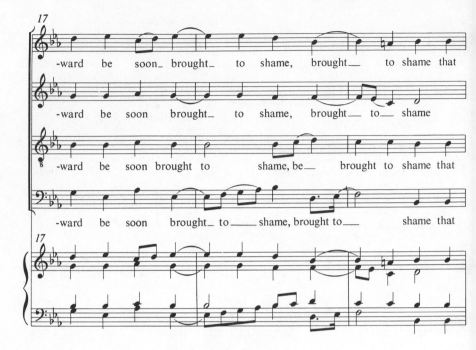

But let all those that seek thee be joy-ful and glad in

But let all those that seek thee be joy-ful and glad in

But let all those that seek thee be joy-ful and glad in

But let all those that seek___ thee be joy-ful and glad in___

thee,   and let all such as de-light in thy sal - va - ti - on

thee,   and let all such as de-light in thy sal - va - ti - on

thee,   and let all such as de-light in thy sal - va - ti - on

thee,   and let all such as de-light in thy sal - va - ti - on

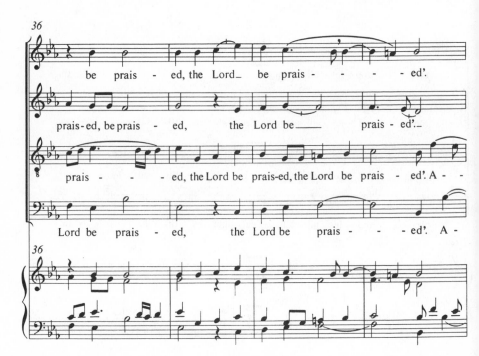

40

EDITORIAL NOTE

1. Sources:
A. Barnard's **First Book of Selected Church Music** 1641.
B. British Museum; Add. Ms. 30478 *c.*1665.
C. Durham Cathedral; Mss. C 14, C 15 and C 19 *c.*1670.
D. Wimborne Minster; Alto, Tenor & Bass Part-Books *c.*1670.
(No Shelf Marks)
E. York Minster; The Decani books of The 'Gostling' Set *c.*1675.

2. Editorial practice:
Cautionary accidentals in brackets, crossed slurs and the organ part are editorial.

3. Variants:
Another and presumably earlier version of this anthem is to be found in Barnard's manuscript part-books, Royal College of Music Mss. 1045-1051, which date from c. 1625. The setting is substantially longer than the present edition, breaking into triple metre for the setting of the words 'joyful and glad'. The editor has confined his attention here to revising the version of Tudor Church Music 78 edited by Percy C. Buck.

Source	/ bar	/ stave	/ beat	/ variant
D	/ 3	/ 2	/ 4	/ ♩.D ♩E
D	/ 5	/ 3	/ 1–2	/ ♩.C ♪D
D	/ 5	/ 2	/ 3–4	/ ♩ ♪ ♪
D	/ 10	/ 2	/ 1–2	/ ♩.G ♪F
D	/ 10	/ 4	/ 3–4	/ ♩ ♩
D	/ 11	/ 4	/ 4	/ ♮ to A
D	/ 13	/ 2	/ 1–4	/ ♩G ♩F
D	/ 16	/ 3	/ 4½	/ ♮ to A
D	/ 18	/ 2	/ 2	/ ♩G ♩A♭
D	/ 20	/ 3	/ 3–4	/ ♩A ♩B♭
D	/ 23	/ all parts	/	/ no pause mark
D	/ 25	/ 4	/ 4½	/ last quaver B♭
D	/ 39	/ 3	/ 3–4	/ ♩B♭ ♩F ♩E♭
A	/ 41	/ 4	/ 3–4	/ ♩ ♫

16. HOW GOODLY ARE THY TENTS

Numbers XXIV, vv. 5, 6

F. A. GORE OUSELEY
(1825-1889)

This anthem may be performed first as a quartet and then repeated in chorus.

Expression marks in bars 30, 35-37 are editorial.

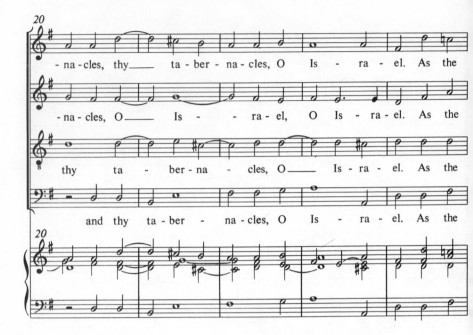

-na-cles, thy___ ta - ber - na-cles, O Is - ra - el. As the

-na-cles, O___ Is - - ra - el, O Is - ra - el. As the

thy ta - ber - na - cles, O___ Is - ra - el. As the

and thy ta - ber - na - cles, O Is - ra - el. As the

val - leys are they spread forth: as gar - dens by___ the ri - ver

val - leys are they spread forth: as gar - dens by the ri - ver

val - leys are they spread forth: as gar - dens by___ the ri - ver

val - leys are they spread forth: as gar - dens by___ the ri - ver

side; as the val - - leys are they spread forth: as

side; as the val - - leys are they spread_ forth: as

side; as the__ val - leys are they spread forth: as

side; as the val - - leys are they spread forth:__ as

gar - dens by__the ri - ver side.__

gar - dens by the ri - ver side, by the__ ri - ver_ side.

gar - dens by__the ri - ver side, by the__ ri - ver_ side.

gar - dens by__ the ri - - - ver side.

17. I SAT DOWN UNDER HIS SHADOW

Song of Solomon II, vv.3,4

EDWARD C. BAIRSTOW
(1874-1946)

This anthem is published separately (O.U.P. A4).

© Oxford University Press 1925

18. LEAD ME, LORD

S. S. WESLEY
(1810-1876)

Psalm 5, v.8; 4, v.9

from *Praise the Lord, O my soul*

The four bars of introduction are editorial and optional.

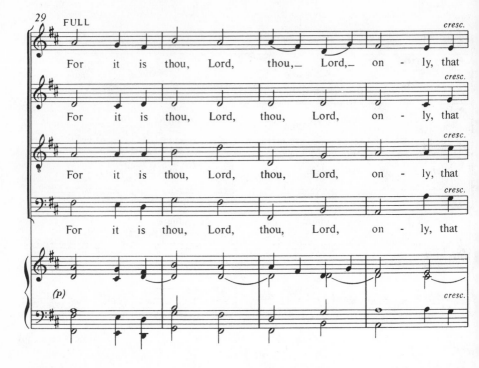

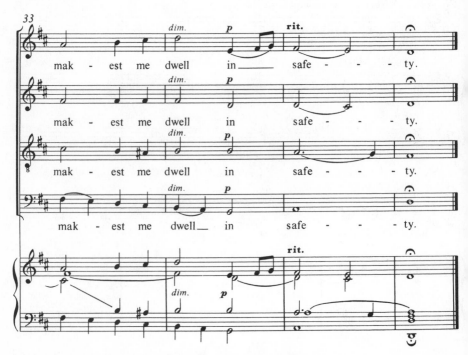

19. LIFT UP YOUR HEADS, O YE GATES

Psalm 24, vv. 7-10

WILLIAM MATHIAS
(Op. 44, No. 2)

The Lord strong and migh-ty, the Lord strong and migh-ty, the

Man.

Lord migh-ty in bat-tle.

Lift up your heads, O ye gates,

Man.

Ped.

lift up your heads, O ye gates, — ev - en lift them up, ye ev-er-last-ing doors,

ff

and the King of glo - ry — shall come in. —

Who is this King of glo-ry?
p

Who is this King of glo-ry?
p

mp Who is this King of glo-ry?

mp Who is this King of glo-ry?

p

mp

Ped.

20. LET MY PRAYER

Edited by ANTHONY GREENING

JOHN BLOW
(1649-1708)

Source: R.C.M. Ms 1097 – a full score dated 1802 in the hand of William Horsley.

The keyboard reduction and marks of expression are editorial.

lift - ing up of my hands be as   an even-ing   sac - ri - fice,   let the lift -

lift - ing up   of my hands   be   as   an even-ing sac - ri - fice,   let the

lift - ing up   of my hands   be   as   an even - ing   sac - ri-fice,   let the

lift - ing up   of my hands   be   as   an even - ing   sac - ri-fice,   let the

- ing up   of my hands be as   an   even - ing sac - ri - fice.

lift - ing up   of my hands   be   as   an   even-ing sac - ri - fice.

lift - ing up   of my hands   be   as an even - ing   sac - ri - fice.

lift - ing up   of my hands   be   as   an even - ing sac - ri - fice.

21. LO, GOD IS HERE

JOHN WESLEY (1739) from the
German of G. Tersteegen (1729)

FRANCIS JACKSON
(Op. 36, No. 5)

* orig:—'dreadful'

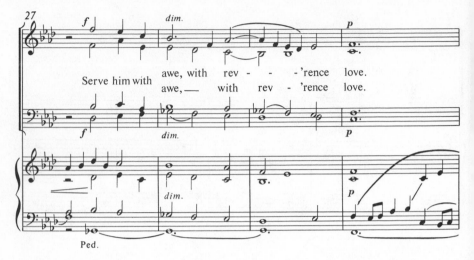

Serve him with   awe, with   rev – – –'rence   love.
                  awe, —— with   rev – 'rence   love.

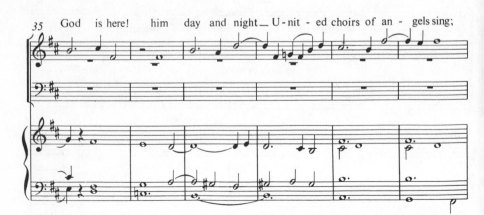

God   is here!   him   day and night— U – nit – ed choirs of an – gels sing;

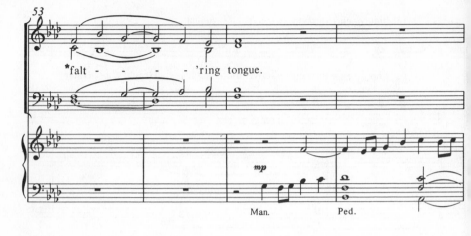

*falt - - - - 'ring tongue.

Man.   Ped.

Be - ing of be - ings!   Be -

cresc.   Man.

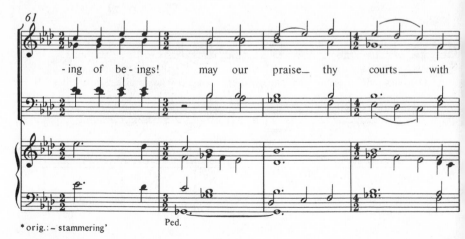

-ing of be - ings!   may our   praise___ thy   courts___ with

Ped.

* orig.: – stammering'

grate - ful fra-grance fill;   Still _ may _ we _

stand be-fore _ thy _ face, Still _ hear   and   do   thy   sov - reign

Still do _____ thy sov - - reign

will;   To thee _ may all _____ our thoughts a - rise,

will;

Man.   Ped.   Man.

Cease - less, _____ ac - cept -

- - - ed _____ sa - cri - fice.

22. LORD, I TRUST THEE

Edited by DENYS DARLOW

G.F. HANDEL
(1685-1759)

Lord, I trust thee, I a - dore thee,

Ah! thou friend of man, re - store me!

From *The Passion of Christ* (1716) edited by Denys Darlow (O.U.P.) The text is translated from the original German. Expression marks in brackets are editorial.

This anthem is published separately (O.U.P. E110).

© Oxford University Press 1965

On thy lov - ing— grace— re - ly - - ing,

For the bread— of life— I'm sigh - ing.

Quench my thirst and let— my hun - ger— cease,

Fill my heart with joy and end - less peace.

When the breath of life has left me,

May my soul be blend - ed with thee.

23. LORD THAT DESCENDEDST, HOLY CHILD

ERIC MILNER-WHITE

ERIC GRITTON

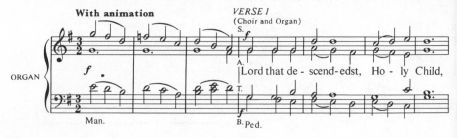

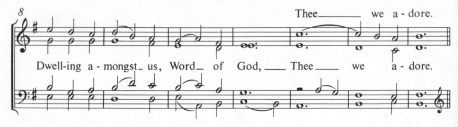

Words from *My God, my Glory* by permission of The Society for Promoting Christian Knowledge.

Thee_____ we a - dore.

-me - ga, God_ of Gods, Thee_____ we a - dore.

VERSE 6

VOICES IN UNISON

6. Lord ev - er - bless - ed, God_ most high,

ORGAN

Ped.

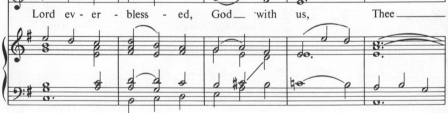

Lord ev - er - bless - ed, God_ with us, Thee_____

rit.   ff

_ we a - dore, Thee_____ we a - dore.

ff

24. MOST GLORIOUS LORD OF LYFE!

Words by
EDMUND SPENSER

DAVID LORD

So let us love, deare Love, _____ lyke as we ought, Love

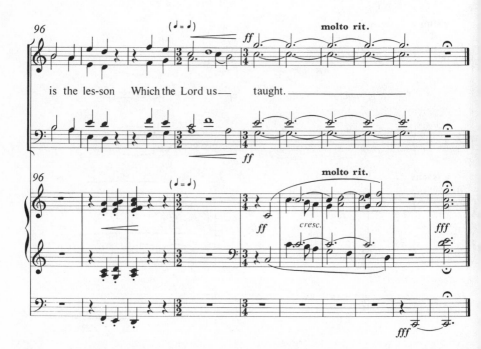

is the les-son Which the Lord us_ taught. _____

25. NOT UNTO US, O LORD

Psalm 115, v.1

T. A. WALMISLEY
(1814-1856)

The small notes in the alto part are in the original but may be omitted, in which case editorial small notes in the tenor part should be used where provided.

Bar 22, beat 3, Alto: *cresc.* in orig.

26
Lively
(f)
truth's, thy truth's sake. Hal - le - lu - jah! Hal - le - lu - jah!
truth's, thy truth's sake. Hal - le - lu - jah! Hal - le - lu - jah!
truth's, thy truth's sake. Hal - le - lu - jah! Hal - le - lu - jah!
truth's, thy truth's sake. Hal - le lu - jah! Hal - le lu - jah!
33
p
Hal - le - lu - jah! Hal - le - lu-jah! Hal - le - lu - jah!
Hal - le-lu-jah! Hal - le - lu-jah! Hal-le - lu - jah!
Hal - le - lu - jah! Hal - le - lu-jah! Hal-le - lu - jah!
Hal - le - lu - jah! Hal - le - lu - jah! Hal - le - lu - jah!

*orig. B

Hal - le - lu - jah! Hal - le - lu - jah! Hal - le - lu-jah!

Hal-le - lu - jah! Hal - le - lu - jah! Hal - le - lu- jah! Hal-

Hal-le - lu - jah! Hal - le - lu - jah! Hal - le - lu-jah!

Hal - le - lu - jah! Hal - le - lu - jah! Hal - le - lu-jah!

Hal - le - lu-jah! Hal-le - lu-jah! Hal - le - lu - jah!

- - le-lu-jah! Hal - - - - le-lu - jah!

Hal - le - lu-jah! Hal - le - lu-jah! Hal - le - lu - jah!

Hal-le - lu-jah! Hal - le - lu-jah! Hal - le - lu - jah!

'Composed Octr 5th 1844'

26. O ALMIGHTY GOD

Edited by ANTHONY GREENING

GEORGE BARCROFTE
(fl. c. 1600)

Collect for the 2nd Sunday after the Epiphany, B.C.P.

Sources: Ely Cathedral – MS. 28 (Tenor part-book c. 1670)
MS. 5 (Vocal score c. 1690)
B.M.–Harl. MS. 7340

Editorial Practice: Bar lines, crossed slurs, and the keyboard reduction are editorial.

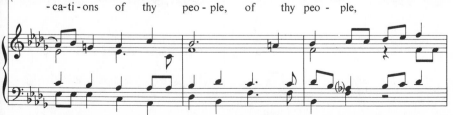

*editorial

all the days of our_____ life, all the days of our____

of our life, all the days, all the days of

life, all the days of our life, all the days of

life, all the days of our____ life, all the days of_ our_

_____ life; through Je - -

our life; through Je - - sus Christ our Lord, through

our life; through Je - - sus Christ__ our Lord, through

____ life; through Je - sus Christ our Lord, through

27. O CHRIST, O BLESSED LORD

T. KINGO
Tr. A.J. MASON

RICHARD WAGNER
(1813-1883)

Adapted by the Editor from *The Mastersingers*, Act 3, Scene 5. Original key G.
Words slightly adapted from *Hymns Ancient and Modern Revised* by permission.

28. O CHRIST, WHO ART THE LIGHT AND DAY

Edited by FRANCIS JACKSON
Tr. W. J. Copeland and others

ROBERT WHYTE
(d. 1574)

Source: British Museum add. Mss. 18936-9: Part books ff. S., A., B., 25., T., 7.
A secondary source, in lute tablature (Add. Ms. 29246 f.44), confirms the
editorial accidentals relating to *musica ficta*.

Editorial Procedure: Barring has been modernized and note values halved; the
original pitch is retained. The time signature, small accidentals, and the
organ part are editorial.

Text: The words (from *The English Hymnal*) have been added by the editor; the
original Latin, beginning **Christe qui Lux es et Dies,** is not written out in
the Mss.

29. O COME, YE SERVANTS OF THE LORD

(LAUDATE NOMEN DOMINI)

Edited by ANTHONY GREENING

CHRISTOPHER TYE
(c.1500-1572 or 1573)

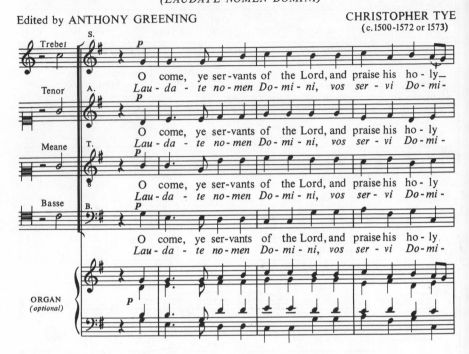

1. Source:

The music of this anthem is taken from Tye's *Actes of the Apostles*, which was published in London in 1553. The four voice parts are all contained in a single small volume. The original text for the music was a metrical version of Chapter 4 of the Acts, beginning:

'When that the people taught they had
There came to them doutles
Priests and rulers as men nye mad
And eke the Saduces,
Whome it greved that they should move
The people and them leade
That Jesus Christe by powre above
Should ryse up from the deade'.

2. Editorial Practice:

Barring and suggested dynamics are editorial, as well as the keyboard accompaniment – (the title page of the work mentions lute participation). The text which has come to be associated with the music was originally published in the 19th century; the first half is a rhyming paraphrase of vv. 1 and 3 of Psalm 113. In accordance with other modern editions of this adaptation, repeat marks, which are not in the source, have been added to make the work into an anthem of acceptable length. However, it should be noted that 'directs' in the voice parts indicate that *all* the music (without the repeats) was to be re-used for the ensuing stanzas of the Chapter.

* B in original

30. O GOD, WHO BY THE LEADING OF A STAR

Edited by
ROBIN LANGLEY

THOMAS ATTWOOD
(1765-1838)

Source: *Attwood's Cathedral Music . . . Edited, and the Organ Accompaniment arranged, by Thomas Attwood Walmisley;* Ewer, London (1852). Attwood's note-values have been halved and slurs modernised; crossed slurs, small notes and accidentals, and symbols in [ ] are editorial. The original organ accompaniment has been retained despite its use of the old GG compass.
Text: Collect for Epiphany, B.C.P.

on - ly be-got-ten Son to_ the_ Gen - tiles, mer - ci-ful - ly

on - ly be-got-ten_ Son to the Gen- tiles, mer - ci-ful-ly

on - ly be - got-ten_ Son_to the Gen- tiles, mer - ci-ful - ly

on - ly be-got - ten Son to the Gen- tiles, mer - ci-ful - ly

grant that we which know thee now by faith may af - ter this

grant that we which know thee now by faith may af - ter this_

grant that we which know thee now by faith may af - ter this

grant that we which know thee now by faith

31. O GOD MY KING

Edited by ANTHONY GREENING

JOHN AMNER
(1579-1641)

Psalm 145 : vv. 1, 3, 8 and 21.

Editorial note: This anthem is extant in only two manuscript sources — Ely Cathedral Ms 4 (an organ score) and Ms 28 (a tenor part-book). It is offered here as a conjectural reconstruction.

Editorial practice: Small accidentals, small notes, cautionary accidentals in brackets, crossed slurs, dynamics, and words in square brackets are editorial.

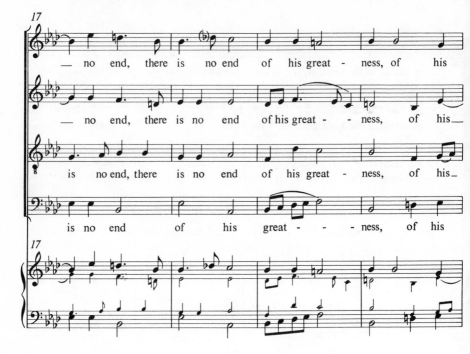

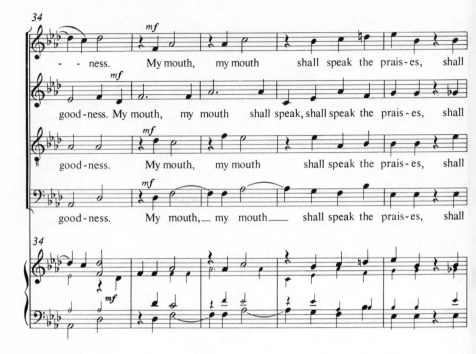

32· O GOD THE KING OF GLORY

Edited by
FRANCIS JACKSON
Collect for Sunday after
Ascension Day, B.C.P.

HENRY PURCELL
(1659-1695)

Source: The 'Gostling' part-books in York Minster Library

Small accidentals, cautionary accidentals in brackets, tempo and dynamic indications, dotted barlines, and the keyboard reduction are editorial.

1) MS. has 'into'   2) ♯ repeated in MS.

3) 'whither' in soprano only in MS.   4) ♩ ♩ = ○ in MS.   5) D♯♩ = ○ in MS.

33. O FOR A CLOSER WALK

Words by
W. Cowper (1731-1800)

Melody: Scottish Psalter, 1635
arranged by C. V. STANFORD (1852-1924)

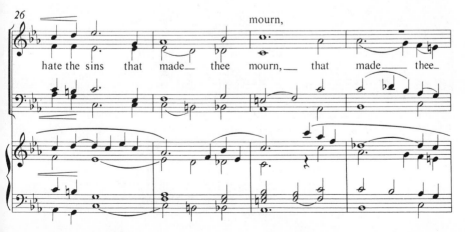

So pur-er light shall mark the road

That leads me *dim.* to

That leads me to the Lamb.

34. O PRAY FOR THE PEACE OF JERUSALEM

Psalm 122, vv. 6-8

JOHN GOSS
(1800-1880)

* orig.: ♪ = 100
from *Praise the Lord, O my soul*

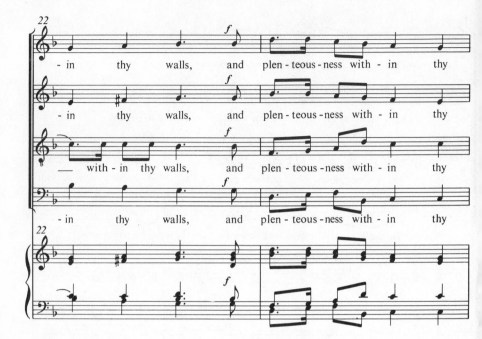

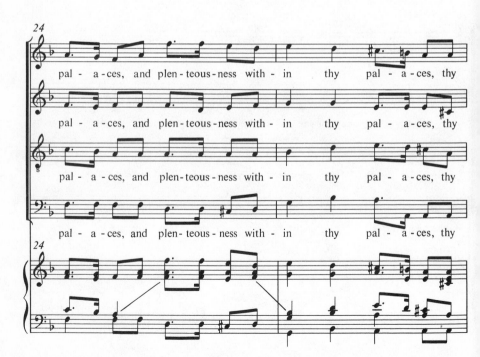

35. O STRENGTH AND STAY

Ascribed to ST. AMBROSE, 340-97
Translated from the Latin
by ELLERTON & HORT

Melody composed or adapted by L. BOURGEOIS
for the Genevan Psalter, 1543
arranged by W. H. HARRIS

* A reed stop of plaintive quality is suggested, such as vox humana (without tremulant), schalmei, or oboe.

co - e - ter - nal Word,   Who, with the Ho - ly__ Ghost, by all things

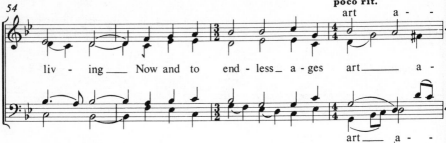

poco rit.

liv - ing __ Now and to   end - less __ a - ges   art __   a -

art __ a -

a tempo

- dored. A - - - - - - - - - men. __

S.

- dored.   A - - - men. __

A.

- dored. __   A - - - - - - - men. __

T.

- dored.   A - - - - - - - - men.

- dored. A - - men,   A - - - men. __

B.

- dored.   A - - - - - - - men. __

a tempo

p

Ped. only

To Canon H. Norman Hodd and the Choir of Mansfield Parish Church

36. O TRINITY, MOST BLESSED LIGHT

? ST. AMBROSE (340-97)
Tr. J. M. Neale and others

C. KENNETH TURNER

fi -ery sun de - parts,__ Shed thou thy beams with - in our hearts.

sun____ de - parts,

Sw. *p legato espress.*

SOPRANOS

pochiss. rall.   a tempo   **Con moto**   *mp*

ALTOS

To   thee__ our morn - ing song of praise,__

mp

pochiss. rall.   a tempo   **Con moto**
Voices only

SOPRANOS

SOPRANOS
mf

Thee may our

TENORS & BASSES
mp

ALTOS

To   thee   our   even - ing   prayer_ we raise,

legato

Man.

cresc.

Ped.

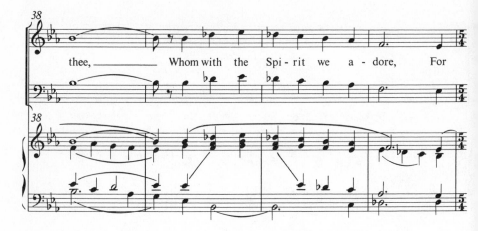

thee, _____ Whom with the Spi - rit we a - dore, For

ev - er, for ev - er, for ev - er and_ for ev - er -

-more.   A - - - - men.

37. O VOS OMNES

(O MY PEOPLE)

Edited by DENYS DARLOW

Lamentations 1, v. 12

CARLOS CORREA
(1680 - c. 1747)

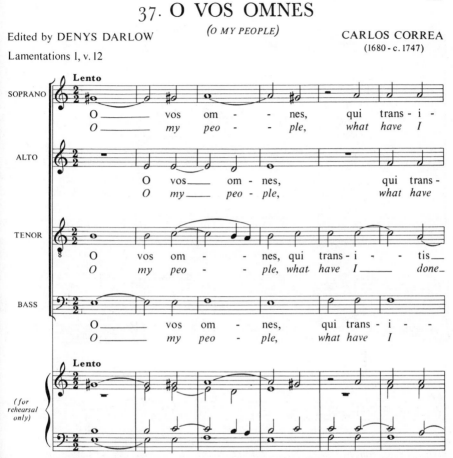

Enrique Carlos Correa was born in Lisbon, and studied music with Father Domingos Nunes Pereira. In 1746 he took the religious habit of the Santiago order and became Chapel-Master of the cathedral in Coimbra. He wrote numerous compositions for the church.

Source: Manuscript from the Santa Cruz Monastery, Coimbra, Portugal.

Editorial practice: The tempo indication, small accidentals, cautionary accidentals in brackets, and the keyboard reduction are editorial. The underlay is clearly shown in the manuscript, and it has not been thought necessary to indicate editorial slurs.

It is apparent from the source that a number of note-values were incorrectly copied: these obvious errors have been corrected.

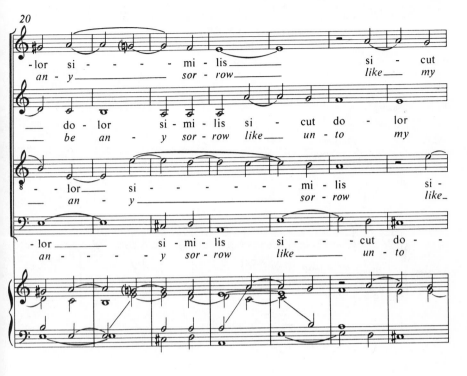

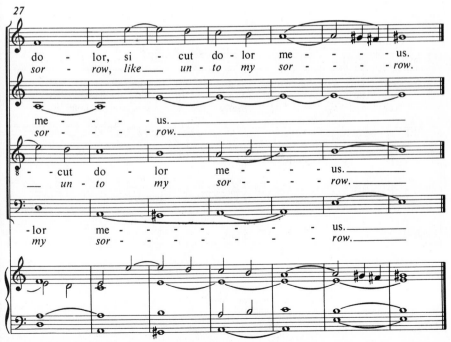

38. OF THE FATHER'S HEART BEGOTTEN

CORDE NATUS EX PARENTIS

(A Christmas hymn)

Melody from 'Piae Cantiones,
Theoderici Petri Nylandensis', 1582
arranged by
DAVID WILLCOCKS

Prudentius (*b*. 348)
Tr. R. F. DAVIS

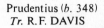

1. Of the Fa - ther's
3. He as - sumed this
5. This is he, whom

heart be - got - ten, Ere the world from cha - os rose,
mor - tal bo - dy, Frail and fee - ble, doomed to die,
seer and sy - bil Sang in a - ges long gone by;

Words reprinted by permission of J. M. Dent & Sons, Ltd.
This anthem is published separately (O.U.P. E100)

© Oxford University Press 1963

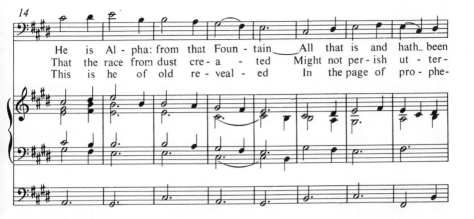

14

He   is   Al - pha: from that Foun - tain____All   that   is   and   hath_ been
That   the race from dust cre - a - ted   Might not per - ish   ut - ter-
This   is   he   of   old   re - veal - ed   In   the page of   pro - phe-

22

flows;   He   is   O - me - ga,   of   all_____ things__Yet to
- ly,   Which the dread -ful Law had sen - - - tenced   In   the
- cy;   Lo! he comes, the pro - mised Sa - - - viour;   Let the

after vv. 1 and 3: straight on for vv. 2 and 4
after v. 5: to p. 169 for v. 6

30

come the mys - tic Close,
depths of hell   to   lie,   *Ev - er-more and ev - er - more.___*
world his prais - es   cry!

VERSES 2, 4

SOPRANOS (and ALTOS)

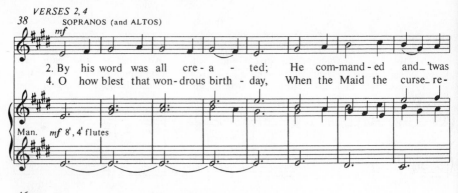

2. By his word was all cre - a - ted; He com-mand - ed and_ 'twas
4. O how blest that won - drous birth - day, When the Maid the curse_ re-

Man. *mf* 8', 4' flutes

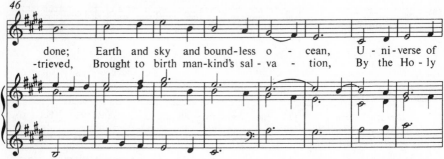

done; Earth and sky and bound-less o - cean, U - ni-verse of
-trieved, Brought to birth man-kind's sal - va - tion, By the Ho - ly

three_ in one, All that sees the moon's soft ra - - - diance,
Ghost con-ceived; And the Babe, the world's Re - deem - - - er,

D.S. for vv. 3 and 5

All that breathes be-neath the sun, *Ev - er- more and ev - er - more.__*
In her lov - ing arms re-ceived,

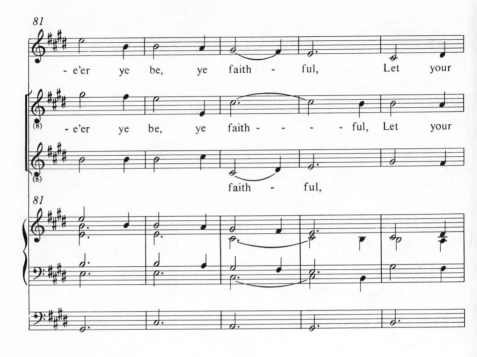

-e'er ye be, ye faith - ful, Let your

-e'er ye be, ye faith - - - ful, Let your

faith - ful,

joy - ous an - thems ring, Ev - 'ry tongue his name con-

joy - ous an - thems ring,___ Ev - 'ry tongue his

- fess - - - - ing,   Count - less voi - ces an - swer-

name con - fess - - ing, ____ Count - less voi - ces an - swer-

- ing,   Ev - er - more   and   ev - er - more. ____

Ev - er, ev - er - more.

- ing,   Ev - er - more   and   ev - er - more.

Ev - er, ev - er - more.

Ev - er - more   and   ev - er - more.

Tuba

39. THE LORD'S PRAYER

Edited by
ANTHONY GREENING

ROBERT STONE
(1516-1613)

Also available separately (A305)

8

And let us not be led in - to temp - ta - ti - on;
lead us not

* Omit the notes within brackets
when italic text is used.

9

but de - li - ver us from all evil. A - - - men.
e - vil.

1. **Sources:**
    A Bodleian Library, Oxford; MSS Mus sch e 420-422 c. 1548
    B John Day's *Certaine Notes* 1560 & 1565

2. **Editorial Practice:**
    Crossed slurs, the small accidental, and text in italics are editorial.

3. **Variants:**

Source	/	bar	/	stave	/	beat	/	variant
B	/	2	/	all vv	/	1-3	/	three crotchets for 'hallowed'
B[1560]	/	4	/	1	/	13	/	F for 'in'
A	/	7	/	4	/	15-16	/	low F also
B	/	8	/	all vv	/	13-14	/	crotchet, minim
B	/	9	/	all vv	/	8	/	'all' omitted
B	/	9	/	all vv	/	10	/	ꞇ minim
B	/	9	/	1	/	11-12	/	crotchet A, crotchet F
A	/	9	/	4	/	10	/	no flat to E
B	/	9	/	all vv	/	No repeat mark		

The pause marks are from A—the barlines from B

4. **Pitch:**
    This setting was written for men's voices—AATB. It is here presented for
    SATB; and can be sung a tone or a minor third higher. If performed by men,
    it can be sung a tone lower.

40. PRAISE THE LORD, YE SERVANTS

Edited by BRUCE WOOD

JOHN BLOW
(1649-1708)

Psalm 113, vv. 1 and 2

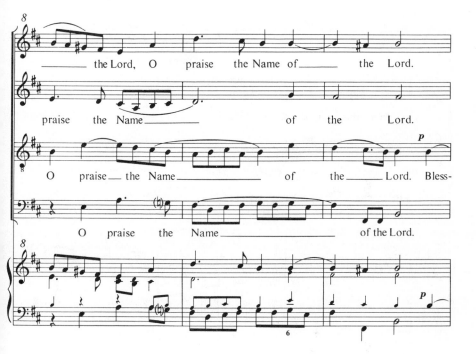

the Lord, O praise the Name of_____ the Lord.

praise the Name_____ of the Lord.

O praise_ the Name_____ of the_____ Lord. Bless-

O praise the Name_____ of the Lord.

Bless - ed, bless - ed be the Name_ of the Lord:

Bless - ed, bless - ed be the Name_of the Lord:

- -ed, bless - ed be the Name of_____ the Lord: from

Bless - ed, bless - ed be the Name of_____ the Lord: from

from this time forth for
from this time forth for ev - er - more, from
this time forth for ev - er - more, for ev - er - more, for
this time forth for ev - er - more,

ev - er - more, from this time forth for ev - er -
this time forth for ev - er - more, from this time forth for
ev - er - more, from this time
from this time forth for ev - er - more, from

this_time forth____ for ev - er - more, for ev - er - more.

from this time forth for ev - er - more, for ev - - - er- more.

ev - er-more, from this_time forth_for_ ev - er - more.

forth_for ev - er - more, for ev - - - - er - more.

Editorial Note

Sources:

A B.M. Add. MS 17,839 ⎱
B B.M. Add. MS 30,932 ⎰ : 18th-century scores with organ bass.
C Tenbury MSS 797-803: seven part-books (lacking Medius Cantoris) in the hand of John Gostling (ca. 1650-1733).
D Tenbury MSS 1176-1182: four part-books (lacking four more, one of each voice) and three-volume organ book, in the same hand as C.
E Fitzwilliam MS 116: holograph organ book, 1700 or later.

Editorial procedure:
Readings of C and D for the voices (except where noted), and of E for the organ part, are preferred. A few rests preceding new entries in the organ part have been replaced by editorial in-filling. Obvious errors are corrected silently. Barring, small notes and rests, small accidentals, monitory accidentals in round brackets, and . all dynamic markings are editorial.

Variant readings:
4 Tenor 4: B (A, B, C, D).
8, 9 Tenor: melisma on 'praise' instead of 'Name' (C, D).
24 Organ, l.h. 1: tenor note *sb* (D), *m* (E).
27, 28 Tenor: rests omitted (C, D).
29 Alto: 'more' a, *m* (C 799, D).

41. PRAISE TO GOD IN THE HIGHEST

Russian tune
arranged by S.S. CAMPBELL
(Descant by Martin Shaw)

Words translated by A.F.D.

This anthem is published separately (O.U.P.).

The descant and the words are from *The Oxford Book of Carols* and are used by permission of Oxford University Press.

© Oxford University Press 1951

May the truth in its beau-ty flour-ish tri-umph-ant: Praise to

thee. May the good be o-beyed, and e-vil be con-quer'd: Praise

con - quer'd:

Give us laugh-ter, and set us gai-ly re-joic - - -

to thee.

Praise to thee.

Bless_____ us, O Fa - - ther! Praise to_ thee.

Bless_____ us, O Fa - - ther! Praise to_ thee.

Add

Praise to God_ in the high - - est,_ to God!_____

Praise_____ to thee._____

Add full Pedal

42. PRAISE YE THE LORD

Psalm 150 with antiphon

JOHN RUTTER

The rhythmic performance of this piece will be found to be easy if it is remembered that quavers are of constant value and fall into groups of either two or three.

This anthem is published separately (E120)

© Oxford University Press 1969

Praise__ God__ in his ho - li-ness: praise__ him__ in the

Praise   ye   the Lord__

fir - ma-ment of his power.   Praise__   him   in   his

mf legato

Praise   ye   the Lord__

mp

*Small notes are alternatives

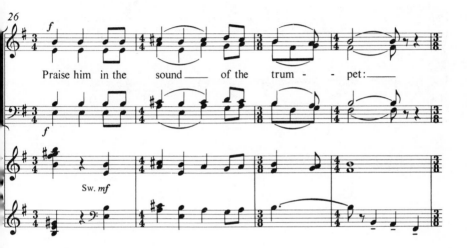

Praise him in the sound___ of the trum - - pet:___

praise   him up - on   the   lute_____   and

Let ev-'ry   thing that hath breath: praise____ the

Lord.____   *Praise ye the   Lord*____   *Praise ye the*

Lord, praise the Lord, praise— ye— the— Lord.—

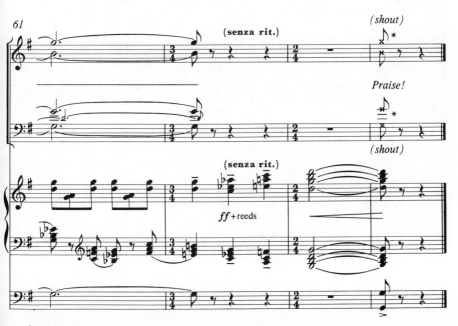

* optional

43. SLEEPERS, WAKE!

MENDELSSOHN
(1809-1847)

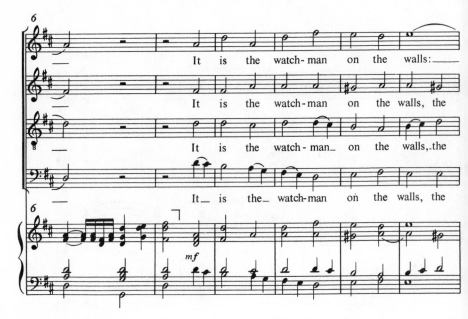

Chorale melody attributed to Philip Nicolai (1556-1608), as arranged by Mendelssohn in his oratorio *St. Paul*.

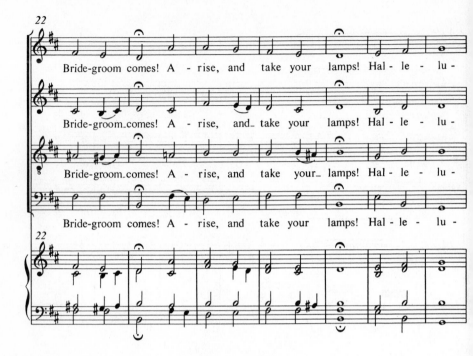

Bride-groom comes! A - rise, and take your lamps! Hal - le - lu -

Bride-groom comes! A - rise, and take your lamps! Hal - le - lu -

Bride-groom comes! A - rise, and take your lamps! Hal - le - lu -

Bride-groom comes! A - rise, and take your lamps! Hal - le - lu -

- jah! A - wake! His king - dom is at hand!

- jah! A - wake! His king - dom is at hand!

- jah! A - wake! His king - dom is at hand!

- jah! A - wake! His king - dom is at hand!

44. TEACH ME, O LORD

Psalm 119, v.33

THOMAS ATTWOOD
(1765-1838)

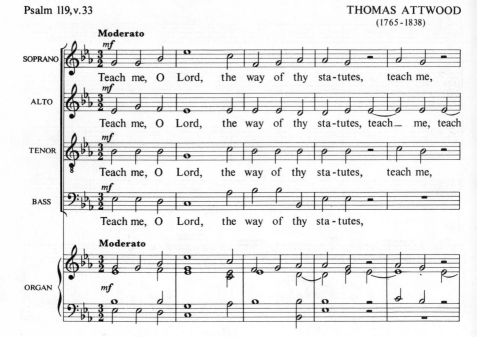

Teach me, O Lord, the way of thy sta-tutes, teach me, teach me, O Lord, the way of thy sta-tutes, teach me, teach me, O Lord, the way of thy sta-tutes, teach me, Teach me, O Lord, the way of thy sta-tutes,

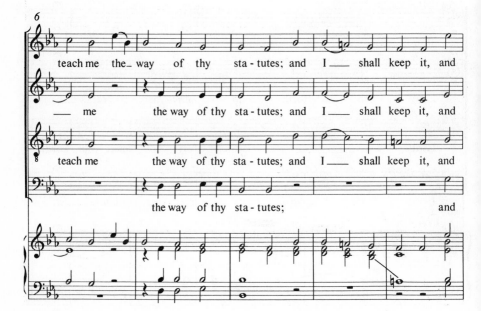

teach me the way of thy sta-tutes; and I shall keep it, and
me the way of thy sta-tutes; and I shall keep it, and
teach me the way of thy sta-tutes; and I shall keep it, and
the way of thy sta-tutes; and

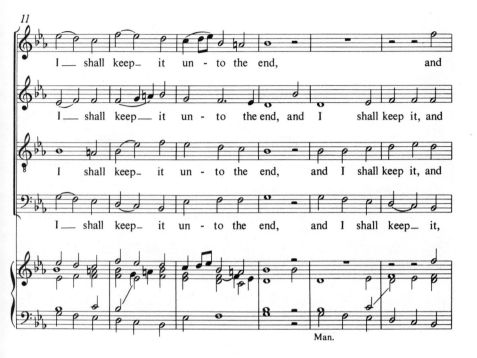

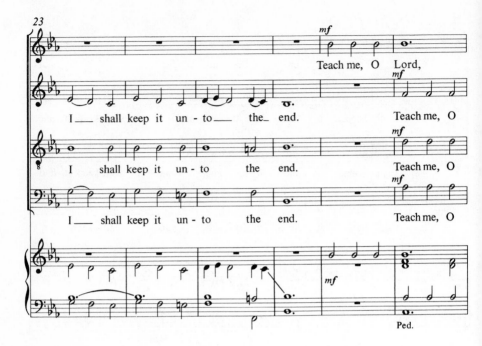

45. THESE ARE THEY WHICH FOLLOW THE LAMB

Edited by FRANCIS JACKSON

JOHN GOSS
(1800-1880)

Revelation XIV, vv. 4, 5

This anthem, dated 1859, first appeared in a collection edited by Ouseley in 1861. Note values have been halved and the organ part slightly modified (a few notes taken from treble to bass stave and vice versa). The only original dynamics are in the organ part at bar 13 and in all parts at bar 18.

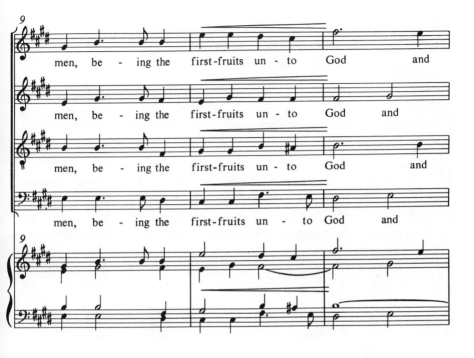

* orig. = 𝅗𝅥. ♩

46. TO THEE, O LORD

Edited and adapted to English words by
A.M. HENDERSON

S. RACHMANINOF
(1873-1943)

Psalm 25, v. 1

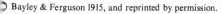

trust in thee. To thee, O Lord, do I lift my soul, my

trust in thee. To thee, O Lord, do I lift my soul, my

trust in thee. To thee, O Lord, do I lift my soul, my

trust in thee. To thee, O Lord, do I lift my soul, my

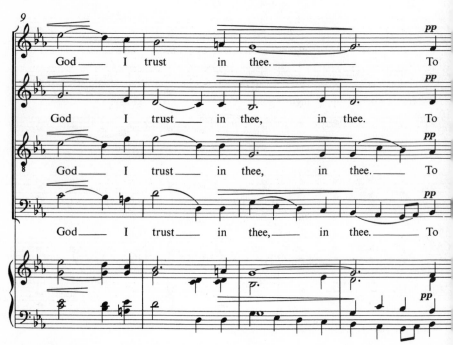

God I trust in thee. To

God I trust in thee, in thee. To

God I trust in thee, in thee. To

God I trust in thee, in thee. To

47. UP, UP! MY HEART! WITH GLADNESS

Words by G.W. DAISLEY

J.S. BACH
(1685-1750)

lights_ our   way!   My_ Sa - viour low_ was laid,   But_ as to   mourn_ we
Christ_ is   free!   Now_his   vic - tor - ious cry   Rings out, and   far___ and
-scrib'd_ in   gold: 'Who_lacked with me_ re - nown,   He_ wears in   heav'n_ the

lights_   our   way!   My Sa - viour low_ was laid,   But   as_ to   mourn_ we
Christ_   is   free!   Now his_ vic - tor - ious cry   Rings out, and   far___ and
- scrib'd   in   gold: 'Who lacked with me_ re - nown,   He   wears in   heav'n_ the

lights_ our   way!   My_ Sa - viour low_ was laid,   But_ as   to   mourn_ we
Christ_ is   free!   Now_his   vic - tor - ious cry   Rings_out,   and   far___and
- scrib'd_ in   gold: 'Who_lacked with me_ re - nown,   He_wears   in   heav'n_ the

lights   our   way!   My Sa - viour low   was laid,   But   as   to   mourn   we
Christ   is   free!   Now his   vic - tor - ious cry   Rings out, and   far   and
-scrib'd   in   gold: 'Who lacked with me   re - nown,   He wears in   heav'n   the

stayed, His   grave_ bonds   did_ he   rend   And to_ the   skies_ as-cend.
nigh He   waves_ his   ban - ners   bright,   Vic - tor - ious   af - ter fight.
crown; Who   chose_with   me_ to   die,   He sits_ with   me_ on high'.

stayed, His   grave_ bonds_____did he rend   And to_ the   skies_as - cend.
nigh He   waves_ his_____ban - ners bright,   Vic - tor - ious   af - ter fight.
crown; Who   chose_with_____me to die,   He sits_ with   me_ on high'.

stayed, His_   grave_ bonds   did_ he   rend   And to   the   skies as - cend.
nigh He_   waves_ his   ban - ners   bright,   Vic - tor - ious   af - ter fight.
crown; Who_   chose_ with   me_ to   die,   He sits   with   me   on high'.

stayed, His   grave_ bonds_did   he   rend   And to__ the_skies   as - cend.
nigh He   waves_ his_ ban - ners   bright,   Vic - tor - ious_ af - ter fight.
crown; Who   chose_ with_ me   to   die,   He sits_ with_me   on high'.

48. VERILY, VERILY I SAY UNTO YOU

Edited by ANTHONY GREENING

St. John, 6, vv. 53-56

THOMAS TALLIS
(? 1505-1585)

1. Sources:
A British Museum: Add Ms. 15166 [Medius] c. 1570
B Peterhouse, Cambridge: Caroline part-books—'former' set—Mss. 34, 38 and 39 c. 1635
C Ely Cathedral: Mss. 1 [Organ] and 28 [Tenor] c. 1670

2. Editorial practice:
Small accidentals, cautionary accidentals in brackets, crossed slurs and barring are editorial.
Spelling has been modernized.

3. Pitch:
It may be found more convenient to perform the anthem up a tone.

This anthem is published separately (O.U.P. A247).

© Oxford University Press 1968

49. GOD IS LIVING, GOD IS HERE!

Edited, with English words, by
LAURENCE H. DAVIES

J.S. BACH (1685-1750)
adapted by Franz Wüllner

13
earth his aid; His strong arm, in pow'r - ful fash - ion, All good
eye so clear? When we cry, shall he not heark - en, He who
earth his aid; His strong arm, — in pow'r - ful fash-ion, All — good —
eye so clear? When we cry, — shall he — not heark-en, He — who —
earth his aid; His strong arm, in pow'r - ful fash - ion, All — good —
eye so clear? When we cry, shall he not heark - en, He — who —
earth — his aid; His — strong arm, in pow'r - ful fash - ion, All — good
eye — so clear? When — we cry, shall he — not heark - en, He — who
20
mp cresc.
things — for us hath — made. In his mys - tic ways — pro -
made — the list - 'ning — ear? God is God — the Lord, — all -
things for — us — hath made. In his mys - tic ways — pro -
made the — list - 'ning ear? God is God — the Lord, — all -
things — for us hath made. In — his mys - tic — ways pro-
made — the list - 'ning ear? God — is God the — Lord, all-
things — for us — hath made. In — his mys - tic ways — pro -
made — the list - 'ning ear? God — is God — the Lord, — all -

50. YE CHOIRS OF NEW JERUSALEM

St. Fulbert of Chartres
tr. R. Campbell and others

C. V. STANFORD
(1852-1924)
Op.123

* The registration here is editorial.

Music reprinted by permission of Stainer & Bell Ltd. Words from *Hymns Ancient and Modern Revised*, by permission of the Proprietors.

bursts his chains, Crush-ing the ser - pent's head; _____ And cries a - loud, _____ and cries a - loud _____ through death's do-mains _____ To wake the im - pri - son'd dead.

To wake _____ the im - pri - son'd dead. _____

To wake _____

To wake

*editorial